D0532277

Real Lives
Unsung
Heroes

Fearless Men and Women
Who Changed the World

Toby Reynolds & Paul Calver

BARRON'S

First edition for the United States and Canada published in 2017 by
Barron's Educational Series, Inc.

All inquiries should be addressed to:
Barron's Educational Series, Inc.
250 Wireless Boulevard
Hauppauge, NY 11788
www.barronseduc.com

ISBN: 978-0-7641-6887-1

Library of Congress Control Number: 2016959108

Date of Manufacture: January 2017
Manufactured by: Toppan LeeFung Printing Co., Ltd. Dongguan, China

9 8 7 6 5 4 3 2 1

Please note that every effort has been made to check the accuracy of the information contained
in this book, and to credit the copyright holders correctly. Green Android Ltd apologizes for any
unintentional errors or omissions, and would be happy to include revisions to content and/or
acknowledgments in subsequent editions of this book.

Image credits: www.alamy.com: Stanislav Petrov © Nikolai Ignatiev. www.gettyimages.co.uk:
Patrick Steptoe & Robert Edwards © Pictorial Parade / Staff, Lincoln Beachey © Popperfoto /
Contributor, Rosalind Franklin © Universal History Archive / Contributor, Lincoln Beachey
© Popperfoto / Contributor, Svetlana Savitskaya © SVF2 / Contributor. www.eyevine.com: Omkar
Nath Sharma © Simon de Trey-White / eyevine. www.shutterstock.com: Harvey Milk © Oldrich,
Michael Faraday © Georgios Kollidas, Mary Seacole © catwalker, Arunachalam Muruganantham
© Debby Wong, Wangari Maathai © s_bukley, Sojourner Truth © Everett Historical, Martti
Ahtisaari © thomas Koch. The New York Public Library: Percy Julian © Photos and Prints Division,
Schomburg Center for Research in Black Culture, The New York Public Library, Astor, Lenox and
Tilden Foundations. Oxfam.org.uk: Joe Mitty © Oxfam GB. Australian War Memorial: Vera Deakin
White © Australian War Memorial / Public Domain. Yale University: Beatrice Tinsley © Office of
Public Affairs, Yale University, Photographs of Individuals (RU 686). Manuscripts and Archives,
Yale University Library. Wikimedia Commons: Henrietta Lacks © Harvard University, Irena Sendler
© Harvard University, Alan Turing © Jacek Halicki / Public Domain, Barbara McClintock
© Smithsonian Institution / Science Service; Restored by Adam Cuerden, Asa Philip Randolph
© John Bottega, NYWTS staff photographer, Mary Anning © sedgwick museum / B. J. Donne,
George Washington Carver © Tuskegee University Archives/Museum / restored by Adam Cuerden,
Nikola Tesla © public domain, Emily Davison © Public Domain, Emmy Noether © Public Domain,
Abbé Pierre © photographed by Studio Harcourt Paris.

Contents

What is an unsung hero?

An unsung hero is one whose deeds and words made the world a better place, but who may have gone unrecognized for these efforts or been forgotten about over time. Perhaps his or her work was overshadowed by someone else's or maybe this person deliberately stayed in the background, but in this book the actions of many unsung heroes are brought together to be acknowledged and applauded, and to inspire other generations of humble heroes.

While you may not know the names of the men and women in this book, they all have these things in common—passion and compassion. Some were driven by their passion for an area of expertise—geology, botany, politics, or medicine —others for their message of peace, justice, and equality, but all exhibited compassion. From the quiet dignity of Sojourner Truth, an 18th century African American who peacefully campaigned for women's rights and the abolition of slavery, to

Alan Turing's life saving code-breaking during the Second World War, and Lincoln Beachey's daredevil stunts that showed the world what airplanes were capable of, this book celebrates each life and legacy.

Though their achievements—saving lives, giving life, creating livelihoods, or making life bearable— are extraordinary, these people saw themselves as ordinary, doing what they knew to be right without a thought to their own aggrandizement or safety. They were unassuming, many of them not realizing the significance of their actions nor drawing attention to them. Honors, celebrity, or a place in history were not on their agenda.

Thankfully there are like-minded people doing the extraordinary today that may save millions of lives or make the life of one person better. No matter if the deed was big or small, it is to our betterment that they should never be forgotten.

Henrietta Lacks

Born: August 1, 1920, Roanoke, Virginia
Died: October 4, 1951, Baltimore, Maryland

Henrietta Lacks was an African American mother of five, who died from an aggressive strain of cancer when she was only 31 years old.

In January 1951, Henrietta complained of feeling a "knot" inside her. It was assumed that this was a symptom of her pregnancy, but after she gave birth to her fifth child the discomfort continued and she bled profusely. Investigations at the Johns Hopkins Hospital, where she was treated, showed a tumor in her cervix. During the radiation treatments that followed, two samples—a healthy section and a cancerous section—of Henrietta's cervix were removed without permission. The cells were given to Dr. George Gey, a scientist at John Hopkins.

The radiation treatments did not work and Henrietta was admitted to the hospital in August 1951. She remained there until her death in October.

In the meantime, Dr. Gey was studying the cells that had been removed and discovered a remarkable thing. Gey found that the cells could be kept alive and would continue to grow. Up until then, scientists had not managed to keep cultured cells alive in a lab for more than a few days.

Some of the cells from Henrietta's tumor behaved differently: they were able to grow and multiply. This had never been witnessed before. Henrietta's robust and resilient cells, which Gey called HeLa— using the first letters of the donor's names—were to contribute to huge advances in medical research.

In 1954, the HeLa cells were used to develop a vaccination for polio, an infection that was extremely common around the world at the time. In 1955, the cells also became the first human cells to be cloned. Since then, more than 20 tons of HeLa cells have been grown and used for a wealth of medical research, in areas ranging from cancer and AIDS to sensitivities and allergies. The DNA code for the cells has also now been published.

The only dark cloud was that neither Henrietta nor her family gave their permission for the cells to be removed in the first place. Henrietta's family remained unaware of what had happened for a long time. But in 2013, discussions between her family and the National Institute of Health resulted in the Lacks family receiving acknowledgments in scientific papers and being involved with future access to Henrietta's DNA code.

"They became
the first immortal
human cells
ever grown in
a laboratory."

– Rebecca Skloot,
in *The Immortal Life
of Henrietta Lacks*

Stanislav Petrov

Born: September 9, 1939, Odessa, Ukraine

Stanislav Petrov was a lieutenant colonel in the Soviet Air Defense Forces, who is credited to have averted a nuclear war by doing ... nothing!

On September 26, 1983, Stanislav was on duty, monitoring Oko, the Soviet Union's early warning system. Just after midnight, alarm bells sounded to indicate an incoming missile strike from the U.S. This alarm was followed by a second, a third, a fourth, and a fifth. The U.S.-Soviet relationship at this time was very strained, so if he had—as he was trained to do—reported the alert to his superiors, then countermissiles would have been launched by the Soviet Union, however Stanislav correctly declared the alarms to be false.

Later he said that his conclusion was based on a number of factors. This included his belief that an attack from the U.S. would be devised of more than five missiles, and the fact that the system was relatively new and not, in his view, trustworthy. Also, the radar systems on the ground had not picked up any missiles. Stanislav later said that it was his civilian training that had helped him draw these conclusions. He added that he was "fifty-fifty as to whether it was real or a false alarm."

Most of Stanislav's colleagues were military men who were used to following orders and, in his position they would have, without doubt, reported the alarm. Had they done so, it would have resulted in a counterattack on the U.S. by the Soviet Union, and possibly an all-out nuclear war. Stanislav said, "I had obviously never imagined that I would ever face that situation. It was the first and, as far as I know, also the last time that such a thing had happened, except for simulated practice scenarios."

Stanislav was reprimanded for the events of that fateful night—not specifically for what he did, but for mistakes in the logbooks that he was responsible for. Although he says he was promised a reward, he did not receive anything. He was given a new, "less sensitive" post and then took early retirement from the military.

The incident did not become publicly known until the 1990s, when the Soviet Union collapsed. After this, Stanislav received many accolades and awards, including a 2004 World Citizen Award "in recognition of the part he played in averting a catastrophe." He also received a 2011 German Media Award and a 2013 Dresden Prize.

Stanislav Petrov

"They were lucky
it was me on shift
that night."

Irena Sendler

Born: February 15, 1910, Otwock, Poland
Died: May 12, 2008, Warsaw, Poland

Irena Sendler (born Irena Krzyzanowska) was born just outside Warsaw, Poland. She is known for helping to rescue 2,500 Jewish children during the Second World War.

Irena spent her career as a nurse and social worker. When Germany invaded Poland in 1939, she was a senior administrator in the Warsaw Social Welfare Department, which took care of orphaned children, and the poor and the destitute.

In 1942, the Nazis forced Jews to move into the Warsaw Ghetto. Irena joined the Polish Resistance, who helped the British by supplying intelligence and disrupting German supplies. Irena headed the efforts to rescue Jewish children.

In her disguise as a health worker, Irena managed to smuggle babies and children out of the ghetto. She gave them temporary Christian identities and put them into foster homes, orphanages, and convents. She also recorded information about each child, including his or her real name, and buried these notes, stored in jars, in a neighbor's garden. Her plan was that this information would be used to reunite the children to their families.

In October 1943, the Nazis discovered Irena's activities and she was arrested, imprisoned, and brutally tortured. Despite this, she did not reveal any information about fellow resistance workers or the children she had helped. She eventually escaped from prison, returned to Warsaw, and assumed a false name. She started work as a nurse in a public hospital, where she managed to hide a further five Jews from the Nazi occupation. After the war, she was again imprisoned due to her connection with the Polish Resistance.

In 1965, Irena was acknowledged as one of the Polish Righteous in Israel's official memorial to the victims of the Holocaust, but she was not granted permission to travel to Israel to accept the award.

She received no further public recognition until the end of communist rule in Poland. She was then awarded several honors, including three Nobel Peace Prize nominations and the Order of the White Eagle—Poland's highest award given to a civilian. In 2006, the Polish Ministry of Affairs established the Irena Sendler's Award for "Repairing the World." Irena remained in Warsaw until her death at the age of 98.

"Every child saved with my help is the justification of my existence on this Earth, and not a title to glory. Over a half-century has passed since the hell of the Holocaust, but its spectre still hangs over the world and does not allow us to forget."

Alan Turing

Born: June 23, 1912, London, U.K.
Died: June 7, 1954, Cheshire, U.K.

Alan Turing was a pioneering mathematical genius, computer scientist, logician, and cryptanalyst. He had a huge influence on the development of computer science and was key to the Allied victory in the Second World War.

A man of many talents, Alan was an avid cyclist and a marathon runner, with a personal best time of 2 hours and 46 minutes. He almost competed in the 1948 Olympics but an injury prevented him from qualifying. The winning time was just 11 minutes under Alan's, but it was his superior intellect, not his running, for which he became best known.

At the outbreak of the Second World War in 1939, Alan became one of the British government's most successful code-breakers. He cracked the cipher system used on the German Enigma code and generated intelligence that helped the Allies numerous times. This included their success in the Battle of the Atlantic, which effectively shortened the war by some two years.

After the war was over, Alan was based at the National Physical Laboratory, where he designed one of the first stored-program computers.

In 1948, he worked at the University of Manchester, where he became interested in mathematical biology. Then, in 1950, Alan proposed an experiment, which eventually became known as the Turing Test. It tests a machine for intelligent behavior and is still used today. He said that a computer could be said to "think" if a human tester could not tell it apart from a human.

Alan tragically committed suicide in 1954 at the age of just 41 years. This followed years of persecution for his homosexuality and a conviction for "gross indecency." Once he had been revealed as openly homosexual, his security clearance was taken away, so it became difficult for him to do the work he loved. In 2009, the British prime minister, Tony Blair, issued an official public apology for the "appalling way he was treated." In 2013, Queen Elizabeth II also granted him a posthumous pardon.

The A. M. Turing Award is so-named in recognition that Alan was the key founder of theoretical computer science and artificial intelligence. It was first awarded in 1966 and is recognized as the highest award in computer science. It is sometimes called the "Nobel Prize of Computing."

Alan Turing

"A man provided with paper, pencil and rubber, and subject to strict discipline, is in effect a universal machine."

Patrick Steptoe & Robert Edwards

Patrick Steptoe, born: June 9, 1913, Oxford, U.K.
Patrick Steptoe, died: March 21, 1988, Canterbury, U.K.
Robert Edwards, born: September 27, 1925, Batley, U.K.
Robert Edwards, died: April 10, 2013, near Cambridge, U.K.

Steptoe and Edwards were a pioneering gynecologist and physiologist team, who developed the in vitro fertilization process, also known as IVF. This was a radical new way to help infertile couples have children who, prior to the IVF breakthrough, had no possibility of having a baby.

Patrick was an obstetrician and gynecologist with a successful practice in Manchester. He was interested in infertility and became skilled in the use of a laparascope—a thin tube that is used to inspect, diagnose, or perform surgery by accessing organs via tiny incisions into the body. To start he used the laparascope to help treat fertility issues, but in time he developed a technique to safely remove human eggs from ovaries.

Robert, on the other hand, began to study human fertilization in 1960, and by 1968 was able to fertilize a human egg in a laboratory.

In 1966, these pioneering men partnered together to develop a new and revolutionary way to help millions of infertile people have children.

Patrick and Robert spent many years refining their skills until they could grow and nurture human eggs for an optimum time that would better ensure fertilization and development. But they encountered a lot of opposition and were accused of meddling with nature. Religious groups were especially hostile to their research, charging them of trying to "play God." Patrick responded by saying that stopping the research would be like not developing planes because they made bombing possible.

Some of the opposition to their work lessened when, on July 25, 1978, one of their patients gave birth to the first "test tube baby." Louise Brown was a healthy baby girl and was born entirely as a result of in vitro fertilization.

By 2012, more than five million children had been born who only existed because of the work of these remarkable men. The partnership received many awards, but Patrick had already died when the 2010 Nobel Prize for Physiology or Medicine was awarded to Robert in recognition of the development of in vitro fertilization.

"The most important thing in life is having a child. Nothing is more special than a child."
— Robert Edwards

Patrick Steptoe & Robert Edwards

Barbara McClintock

Born: June 16, 1902, Hartford, Connecticut
Died: September 2, 1992, Huntington, New York

Barbara McClintock was a scientist and Nobel Prize-winning pioneer of genetics.

Barbara grew up in Connecticut at a time when marriage was considered more important for a woman than a successful career. However, with a passion for information, she decided to go against the norm and devote her life to research instead.

In 1918, she began studying at Cornell University, New York, and quickly progressed to achieve a Master's and a Ph.D. in botany. Her interest was in plant genetics—the study of a plant's genes—and right after graduation she started research in that area. Whereas most scientists of the time had been analyzing what they could see with the naked eye, Barbara looked even closer at the cells of the plants, revealing far more detail.

In 1931, Barbara started mentoring a student, Harriet B. Creighton. Together, they analyzed the cereal maize and made a big discovery: a process called "chromosomal crossover." Although a similar theory had been proposed 20 years earlier by another scientist, Thomas Morgan, they were the first with solid evidence to prove his ideas.

Barbara continued her research in the years that followed, taking up positions with the University of Missouri and Columbia University. In the 1940s and 1950s, she made a further major discovery—that genes could move around within chromosomes. Scientists had originally thought that genes were in fixed positions on chromosomes.

Although a respected scientist by now—with a place in America's National Academy of Sciences—her new ideas received criticism. She had gathered years of data, yet her work was largely ignored, which led her to stop publishing and presenting lectures on her research. It seemed that her theories were little understood.

It was not until the 1970s, when scientists finally began to verify her discoveries, that her work began to receive its overdue recognition. She was then awarded several honors, including the National Medal of Science from President Richard Nixon and the 1983 Nobel Prize for Physiology or Medicine. Barbara continued to carry out research for the following nine years until her death, clearly demonstrating her passion and commitment for her dedicated work in the laboratory.

Barbara McClintock

"I never thought of stopping, and I just hated sleeping. I can't imagine having a better life."

Asa Philip Randolph

Born: April 15, 1889, Crescent City, Florida
Died: May 16, 1979, New York City, New York

Asa Philip Randolph was a trailblazing American trade unionist and civil rights leader. He was a key figure in the African American civil rights movement. As a child he learned that a person's behavior toward others was more important than the color of their skin. When he grew up, he campaigned tirelessly for justice and equality for African American citizens.

Asa was eager to organize a union for African American workers. In 1925, he founded the Brotherhood of Sleeping Car Porters to stand up against harsh working conditions and low wages. It became the first successful African American trade union in America, gaining more pay, a shorter working week, and overtime pay for its workers.

Asa led many civil rights campaigns, speaking and inspiring vast crowds. He believed in using peaceful mass protest to bring about change. In 1941, he planned to lead thousands of people in a march on Washington, D.C., to protest the discriminatory practices in war-related industries. To prevent this, President Franklin Roosevelt created the Fair Employment Practice Committee. This victory opened up higher paying, skilled jobs to minorities.

After the Second World War, Asa helped to form the League for Non-violent Civil Disobedience Against Military Segregation. The league had several notable successes. Most significantly, it was due to the league's campaign that President Truman banned, in 1948, racial segregation in the armed forces.

In 1963, Asa helped to organize the March on Washington for Jobs and Freedom. For him, it was the realization of a dream when over 200,000 people — both blacks and whites—gathered to support the African American cause. Asa was on the podium when Martin Luther King, Jr., made his "I Have a Dream" speech to the crowd. After the march, Asa said to President Kennedy: "It's going to be a crusade then. And I think that nobody can lead this crusade but you, Mr. President." Asa also contributed to the 1965 "Freedom Budget for All Americans," with its goal of economic justice for all working families.

Asa was central to the civil rights movement in America, and was awarded the Presidential Medal of Freedom. His unstinting determination drove the cause of equality forward, and showed all Americans how non-violent direct action could be effective and change everyone's lives for the better.

Asa Philip Randolph

"A community is democratic only when the humblest and weakest person can enjoy the highest civil, economic, and social rights that the biggest and most powerful possess."

Mary Anning

Born: May 21, 1799, Lyme Regis, U.K.
Died: March 9, 1847, Lyme Regis, U.K.

Mary Anning was a fossil hunter who had an immense influence on the history of science. She grew up and spent her life in Lyme Regis, a seaside town. The beach and cliffs there were full of fossils, and these attracted curious tourists. Mary's family was poor and she and her brother Joseph often collected fossils to sell to visitors.

When Mary was 12 years old, she found the first complete fossil of an ichthyosaur. It was the first in a lifetime of incredible discoveries, some of which were the most important geological finds of all time. Mary didn't go to school, but she taught herself to read and write. She was fascinated by the ancient creatures, their forms preserved in the rocks, and worked hard to learn more about them.

Searching for fossils on the beach was dangerous work. The cliffs above often crumbled, revealing new fossils but crushing anything or anyone below. Mary went fossil hunting after storms, when the wild weather rendered the cliffs most unstable. Though highly risky, it was the best time to spot fossils, and people would pay well for the fossils that the brave collectors found. The money that Mary earned helped support her family.

In 1823, Mary found the first Plesiosaurus fossil. This was followed in 1828 by the first complete pterosaur ever discovered. By this time, Mary had earned enough money to buy a home and a shop, but she continued to study and learn more about her fossils before selling them.

Geologists and fossil collectors from around the world befriended Mary, with many of them approaching her for information and news of her latest research. This, at a time when women were not allowed to vote, let alone attend a university. Thanks to her work, scientists began to understand far more about how life on Earth had developed. Surprisingly, the word "dinosaur," meaning "terrible lizard," only appeared in 1841, almost 30 years after Mary's first major discovery!

Her work was at the heart of a huge shift in our understanding of the natural world, and it may have contributed to Charles Darwin's theory of evolution, which was published shortly after her death. Mary did not seek fame, but this working class woman earned the genuine respect of scientists and the general public. The world owes a great deal to her thirst for knowledge.

"She sells seashells on the sea shore. The shells she sells are seashells, I'm sure. For if she sells seashells on the seashore, then I'm sure she sells seashore shells."

–Tongue-twister inspired by the life of Mary Anning

George Washington Carver

Born: 1864 or 1865 (date unknown), Diamond, Missouri
Died: January 5, 1943, Tuskegee, Alabama

George Washington Carver was a botanist who is best known for his research in and promotion of alternative, nutritious crops. George was born to parents in slavery, who were owned by a couple of small-scale Missouri farmers. A week after his birth, he, his mother, and one sibling were kidnapped. Only George was found. After the abolition of slavery in 1865, he was raised on the farm with his remaining sibling. As a sickly child, he did household duties not manual labor, which gave him time to study the plants on the farm. This interest was a sign of things to come.

In 1896, George earned a Master's degree in Agriculture and established himself as an excellent botanist. He found work leading the agricultural department at an all-black university in Tuskegee, Alabama, and began some pioneering research.

This included developing methods for crop rotation. In this, he proposed that alternating growing cotton with sweet potatoes or soybeans would improve the soil. He also studied overlooked crops, such as peanuts and cowpeas, and discovered and invented hundreds of products, like milk and soap, that could be produced using these legumes.

George's ideas helped poor Southern farmers to improve their crops and income. It was especially important at a time when the country faced economic decline, after years of drought and poor farming practices. Soon, people all over the country sought his advice on new agricultural methods, especially the use of peanuts. George became a national icon for African Americans, and President Theodore Roosevelt asked for his help to improve the quality and yield of the nation's crops.

George rose to fame and toured the country to speak about agriculture, but also used his prominence to promote scientific causes and racial equality. Although he was offered work at many institutions, he preferred to remain working with other African Americans at Tuskegee. He also refused to patent any of his agricultural inventions, believing that they should be freely available.

At the age of 78, George died after falling down a flight of stairs. He came to symbolize how education has the potential to turn anyone's life around. Though born into slavery, he became a symbol of African American achievement, enriching the lives of countless farmers along the way.

George Washington Carver

"Education is the key to unlock the golden door of freedom."

Lincoln Beachey

Born: March 3, 1887, San Francisco, California
Died: March 14, 1915, San Francisco, California

Lincoln Beachey was a world-famous stunt pilot. He helped to invent aerobatics, and earned himself nicknames like "the man who owns the sky," "the world's greatest aviator," and "divine flyer." Beachey said that he felt as safe in the air as on the ground. His skill and confidence made him a hero in the eyes for his millions of fans.

Lincoln first made a name for himself flying airships, but in 1910 he started flying airplanes as part of an exhibition team. Massive audiences came to see his daredevil displays. In June 1911, over 150,000 people watched him perform an exciting display flying over Niagara Falls, sometimes within 20 feet (6 m) of the water.

The young aviator's bravery and quirky sense of humor led to many surprising antics during his stunt flights, including dropping oranges for sportsmen to catch, letting his wheels touch a moving train, and dressing as a woman—complete with silk dress, veil, and sparkly shoes. He was an exemplary showman, and once lost over $300 from his pocket when flying upside down. Alongside these unforgettable moments, he set many new records for speed and altitude.

Lincoln's stunt speciality was the "dip of death," during which he would dive towards the ground at top speed with his arms stretched out. At the last second he would level the plane and zoom down the runway, using his knees to control the landing. In his beloved plane, "Little Looper," he flew as many as 80 loops one after the other.

It was clear to Lincoln that airplanes could be used for more than stunt displays. He campaigned for the government to invest more money in the development of flying for defense and commercial use. In 1914, he carried out a mock attack on the White House to prove that the government was not properly prepared for the new age of aviation. President Wilson was said to have been working in his office when he glanced outside and saw a plane zooming straight toward him.

Lincoln spent his short life doing things that other pilots said were impossible. He died, as he had expected, in the middle of a stunt. He was flying a monoplane when the wings collapsed. The plane fell into San Francisco Bay and he could not free himself from the wreckage. His funeral was said to be the largest that San Francisco had ever known.

Lincoln Beachey

"Instead of being a reckless chance-taker, I am really the pioneer explorer of the uncharted air lanes of the sky . . . I want to open the eyes of the people to the possibilities of the aeroplane."

Omkar Nath Sharma

Born: around 1940, New Delhi, India

Omkar Nath Sharma is a retired blood bank technician who performs an amazing service in Delhi, India. He collects medicines from people who no longer need them and gives them to the poor. His kindness has earned him the nickname "Medicine Baba," which means medicine monk. Omkar's good works have made him famous around Delhi and set an example for everyone in the world.

One day in 2008, a bridge collapsed in Delhi. Many of the injured people died because they were not able to afford the cost of treatment. Omkar was shocked by the unfairness of this. People were dying because they could not afford medicine, and yet richer families had unused medicine sitting on shelves. He was determined to address this situation so all unnecessary deaths could be prevented in the future.

Omkar's idea was simple. He would go from door to door in different parts of Delhi, and ask for donations of unused or unwanted medicines, relying on the willingness of one human to help another. His family were doubtful, worried that it seemed too much like begging, but Omkar was determined that his mission would succeed.

Whenever he is out collecting, Omkar wears a bright orange smock on which is printed his mission and his phone number. At the end of every collection, he carefully records the details of each medicine, and then delivers them to hospitals, clinics, and ashrams that can pass them on to those who need them. Surveys reveal that two-thirds of India's population lack essential medicines.

It is not easy for Omkar to carry out the task he has set himself. His legs were injured in a car accident when he was a child, and this caused the bones to grow deformed, making walking painful. Despite this, he walks up to 3 miles (6 km) every day. Even his bus journeys to and from the slums are made with difficulty.

Omkar dreams of creating a free medicine bank that charities can access, and has even rented a small space in which to securely store some medicines. The Medicine Baba's only payment is his satisfaction in seeing people getting better thanks to him, and beyond that he wants everyone to think before they discard any useful medicines. Omkar is living proof that one person can make a huge difference to the lives of many.

"I will do something to help society."

09250243298
MOBILE MEDICINE
BANK
CONT. No. OMKAR NATH
9250243298, 9971926518
THANKS OR YOUR KIND
CO-ORDINATION
OMAR NATH

Harvey Milk

Born: May 22, 1930, Woodmere, New York
Died: November 27, 1978, San Francisco, California

Harvey Milk was one of the first elected officials in America to be open about the fact that he was gay. He was also a gay rights activist and a passionate civil rights leader, who stood up for those who had no voice in society. He made history and left a lasting legacy.

Harvey realized that he was gay while was still at school, but he did not talk about it. He joined the U.S. Navy, reaching the rank of a Junior Lieutenant, where he served as a diving instructor during the Korean War. He resigned after being questioned about his sexual orientation, and moved to New York, where he made friends with several gay radicals and became involved in politics.

In 1972, Harvey moved to San Francisco and opened a camera shop in the hub of the city's growing gay community. His already ignited interest in political and civic issues increased, especially when he witnessed injustice and discrimination happening around him. He began campaigning to enter politics, and though he failed to win several of the elections he entered, his voice was getting heard and he was developing powerful political connections.

In 1977, Harvey finally won a seat on the San Francisco Board of Supervisors. He was the first openly gay officer that the city had ever had, and one of the first in the U.S. His election made headlines all around the world.

Harvey's election gave hope to oppressed people who were accustomed to facing hostility and prejudice. He was a popular and inspirational supervisor who was admired by many people for being open about his sexuality. He was dedicated to serving everyone in his constituency, and he spoke out on issues that affected poor and voiceless people. His good humor, the fact that he spent time listening to voters, and his rousing speeches gained him huge support.

Tragically, his career and his life were ended too soon. Nearly a year after his election, he was killed by a former city supervisor, Dan White. Like many gay people, Harvey had faced a lot of abuse and hatred. He had received many death threats, but had always refused to let fear dictate what he did. In August 2009, President Barack Obama awarded Harvey Milk the Presidential Medal of Freedom for his contribution to the gay rights movement.

Harvey Milk

Michael Faraday

Born: September 22, 1791, Newington, Surrey, U.K.
Died: August 25, 1867, Hampton Court, Surrey, U.K.

Michael Faraday was a scientist who changed the way we understand the world around us. His experiments and ideas about electricity and magnetism helped to develop the incredible technology we have today. He wrote about electromagnetic rotation, built the first electric motor, and developed the ideas behind electric transformers and generators.

He was born into a poor family, his education was very basic, and he began working for a bookbinder when he was 14 years old. But young Michael was determined to learn, and he started reading the books that were brought in to be bound. The books on scientific subjects, especially electricity, interested him, so it was not long before he attempted simple experiments of his own.

Michael went to four lectures by a famous British chemist called Humphry Davy in 1812, and he was fascinated and made many notes. He was so inspired that he wrote and asked Davy for a job, who sensed something special about this young man. Although the chemist could not offer him a job immediately, a year later Michael became a chemical assistant at the Royal Institution.

Over the next few years, Michael helped scientists with their experiments at the Royal Institution, learning all the time. At last he published his own research, and began to give lectures. He was gaining a reputation as an outstanding scientific mind, and his work on electromagnetic rotation was vital to the development of the electric motor.

Michael was highly respected as a chemist, but he also researched topics that would revolutionize physics and developed new theories about electrochemistry. He helped invent many words that we still use today, such as "electrode" and "ion." Many of the ideas behind later theories of electricity and magnetic fields came from Michael's work. As scientific advisor to Trinity House, his work improved the optical lenses and electric generators used in lighthouses, and in 1858, a world first—the South Foreland lighthouse was equipped with his electric lamp.

In recognition of his research, Michael was given a grace and favor house at Hampton Court, and it was there that he died. Many decades later the great Albert Einstein said that Michael "had made the greatest change in our conception of reality."

Michael Faraday

"Nothing is too wonderful to be true, If It be consistent with the laws of nature."

Mary Seacole

Born: 1805, Kingston, Jamaica
Died: May 14, 1881, London, U.K.

Mary Seacole was a nurse and a heroine of the Crimean War (1853–1856). She came from humble beginnings in Jamaica, but by the time she died her name was known around the world.

She had a Scottish father and a Jamaican mother, but even as a free person of mixed race, Mary had very few civil rights. Her mother, a healer who used herbal remedies, ran a boarding house for injured soldiers and taught Mary all she knew about nursing.

Mary loved traveling, and she was able to visit many countries. Everywhere she went, she learned more about modern medical practices. She became deeply interested in medicine, and healed many people. She married a naval officer, but he died young, and Mary threw herself into her work.

When the Crimean War started, thousands of troops went to fight. Soon there were many wounded soldiers and not enough medical care. Mary wanted to help, so she went to the War Office in London, asking to be sent to the Crimea as an army nurse in Florence Nightingale's team. They refused, but Mary would not give up and she funded her own passage to the Crimea.

Once there, Mary set up the British Hotel where she could care for the wounded. Even though it was dangerous, she also went to the battlefield to care for sick and injured soldiers, using donkeys to carry her supplies. The British troops, always pleased to see her, called her "Mother Seacole."

When the war ended, Mary returned to London. She was poor and ill, but she was well known and people were determined to help as thanks for what she had done in Crimea. This campaign was backed by an equally grateful British army. Mary was declared bankrupt, so a benefit festival and a fund was organized to raise money. Meanwhile, Mary published her memoirs, *The Wonderful Adventures of Mrs. Seacole in Many Lands,* and she was able to live a comfortable life in London, in part due to the monies rasied for her, until her death.

She was awarded the Jamaican Order of Merit in 1991, there is a statue of her at St. Thomas' Hospital, London, and several hospital wards and buildings carry her name. Although some feel that Mary's nursing achievements have been mistakenly promoted over those of Florence Nightingale, this remarkable woman will never be forgotten.

Mary Seacole

"The grateful words and smile which rewarded me for binding up a wound or giving a cooling drink was a pleasure worth risking life for at any time."

Nikola Tesla

Born: July 10, 1856, Smiljan, Austrian Empire (now Croatia)
Died: January 7, 1943, New York City, New York

Nikola Tesla was an inventor whose greatest concept is a fundamental part of radio technology. He helped to develop the alternating-current (AC) electrical system, and discovered the rotating magnetic field. He is appreciated as a true visionary and highly significant in the advancement of science and invention.

Nikola became interested in inventing things as a boy. His mother invented small household appliances, which inspired his interest in science and his fascination with electricity. After he completed his schooling he became an electrical engineer and, in 1884, moved to America, where he worked for the famous inventor, Thomas Edison.

At first the two men worked well together. However, their working relationship broke down and Nikola started to develop an alternative to Edison's direct-current (DC) system. An engineer and industrialist named George Westinghouse noticed Nikola's work, and bought some of his patents for AC power. Soon Westinghouse was in direct competition with Edison, but the AC system won out and went on to become the standard power system used throughout the world.

Nikola continued to come up with new inventions. His "Tesla coil" is still used in modern radio technology, and he also developed ideas that were then used by other innovators for their own inventions. Nikola's demonstrations of electrical experiments were very spectacular, and they earned him a reputation as a stereotypical "mad scientist."

He became increasingly eager to develop the wireless transmission of energy, which would provide every corner of the world with free electricity and communication systems. A group of investors funded him to develop his ideas, but his competitors—one of them being Edison—were ahead of him. Eventually, Nikola was declared bankrupt and had a nervous breakdown.

As Nikola got older, his ideas became more eccentric and he preferred his own company. However, thousands of people attended his state funeral, Nobel Prize winners were the pallbearers, and America's first lady, Eleanor Roosevelt, sent a telegram of condolence. It has been recognized that he was at the heart of the advancement of electrical science, and Nikola's legacy of discovery and invention lives on to this day.

Nikola Tesla

"I do not think there is any thrill that can go through the human heart like that felt by the inventor as he sees some creation of the brain unfolding to success."

Rosalind Franklin

Born: July 25, 1920, London, U.K.
Died: April 16, 1958, London, U.K.

Rosalind Franklin was a chemist and X-ray crystallographer. Her work and legacy are surrounded by claims of underhanded behavior and professional competition. She carried out a lot of the research that led to our understanding of the structure of DNA—the "secret of life."

Rosalind dreamed of being a scientist, and was extremely fortunate in being able to do Physics and Chemistry at school. At this time, it was almost unheard of for females to be taught such subjects. She won a scholarship to Cambridge University, where she studied the natural sciences, and then worked at the British Coal Utilisation Research Association. Here, she studied the porosity of coal—a raw material that was of huge importance to Britain's economy and industry during the Second World War.

Rosalind then spent three years working in Paris, where she became, among other things, a skilled X-ray crystallographer. This tool was used for identifying the atomic and molecular structure of a crystal. So, armed with new skills, she returned to England in 1950 as a research associate at King's College, London, studying DNA fibers.

At King's College, Rosalind met the scientist Maurice Wilkins, and while they had separate DNA projects, they did not get along well and the atmosphere between them grew increasingly more tense, prompting her to move to Birkbeck, University of London, to continue her research.

Rosalind's crystallographic images of DNA stayed at King's College, and gave insights into the molecule's structure that helped others solve the "secret of life." But when the scientists Francis Crick and James Watson, together with Wilkins, published their paper on DNA's structure in 1953, they did not credit Rosalind's contribution or acknowledge how close she had been in 1951–53 to solving the mystery herself.

Rosalind went on to study the structure of the tobacco mosaic virus and the polio virus. In 1956, she fell ill with cancer and died two years later. Only after her death was her role in the discovery of the structure of DNA recognized, and that her experimental data had been used to build the model of DNA. Nevertheless, no amount of intrigue can sully Rosalind's lasting legacy as an inspiring and dedicated scientist of the first rank.

"Science, for me, gives a partial explanation for life. In so far as it goes, it is based on fact, experience, and experiment."

Rosalind Franklin

Svetlana Savitskaya

Born: August 8, 1948, Moscow, Soviet Union

Svetlana Savitskaya was a Soviet cosmonaut who became the second woman to fly into space, and the first woman to fly into space twice. She was also the first woman to do a spacewalk (an extravehicular activity). She has become a great and positive representative of her country.

When she was a teenager, Svetlana started parachuting as a hobby. It became a passion for her, and by the time she was 17, she had done over 450 jumps. She was encouraged to train as a pilot, and attended the best Soviet aviation engineering school. There she became a flight instructor and a test and sports pilot. She set world records in MiG aircraft and team parachute jumping, becoming a world aerobatics champion, and then went on to train as a cosmonaut.

Two years after she started training, Svetlana was chosen as one of the three-person crew for the Soyuz T-7 mission. On August 19, 1982, she became the second woman to fly into space. During the mission, she and the team docked the Soyuz T-7 at the Russian Salyut 7 space station, and Svetlana carried out several experiments on the effects of space travel on the human body.

The next time Svetlana went into space, she became the first woman to complete a second space mission, as well as the first to walk in space. She spent 3 hours and 35 minutes cutting and welding metal outside the vessel. Svetlana earned the Hero of the Soviet Union award twice. She even has two asteroids named after her—4118 Sveta and 4003 Savitskaya. She remained an active cosmonaut until 1993, but she never flew into space again.

She eventually retired from the Russian Air Force as a major, and went into politics. As a committed communist, she was elected as a member of the Russian parliament. She is currently the Deputy Chair of the Committee on Defense.

Svetlana has a long list of honors and awards. Through her work in space and as a politician, she has brought great pride to her country. She was one of the five cosmonauts who raised the Russian flag at the opening ceremony of the 2014 Winter Olympics. She stands as a powerful symbol of her nation's achievements, but more important are her personal accomplishments, here on Earth and in space.

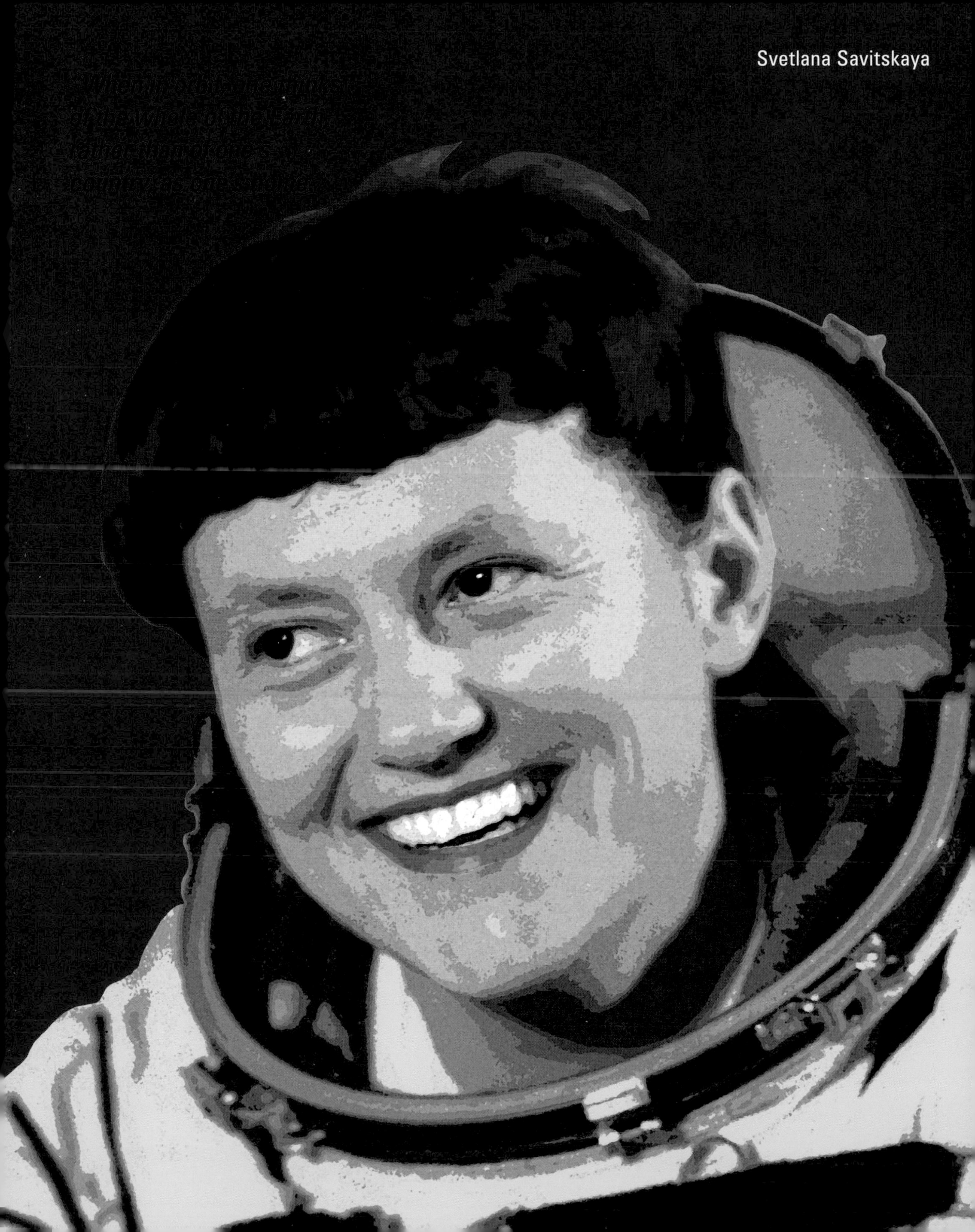

Svetlana Savitskaya

Percy Julian

Born: April 11, 1899, Montgomery, Alabama
Died: April 19, 1975, Waukegan, Illinois

Percy Julian, the grandson of former slaves, overcame barriers of racial segregation to become one of the most influential chemists in U.S. history.

Growing up at a time when U.S. schools would not admit black students once they had completed eighth grade (at age 13), Percy was only able to study Chemistry at DePauw University, Indiana, by taking high school-level evening classes alongside the demands of his course schedule. Despite this, Percy graduated first in his class.

However, impediments to his career followed him throughout his life. Upon completing a Master's degree at Harvard University, he was not allowed to pursue his Ph.D. there due to the color of his skin. Then, when trying to get teaching positions in major universities, he was refused on the basis that white students would not want to be taught by a black instructor. Eventually, he was able to achieve a teaching position at DePauw University, but only after obtaining his Ph.D. in a European university. At DePauw, his first encounter with international fame came when he carried out research and managed to develop, in 1935, a groundbreaking treatment for glaucoma, an eye disease.

The university refused to offer him a professorship for this work because he was black, so Percy eventually went on to work with the Glidden Company. There, he invented a fire-extinguishing foam that saved the lives of countless soldiers in the Second World War. He continued to innovate and research, discovering how to extract drugs, such as progesterone and testosterone, from soybean oil and how to synthesize cortisone so that it was more widely available. This was a significant achievement, as cortisone helps relieve the pain suffered by people with rheumatoid arthritis. After a lifetime's struggle for respect in the scientific field, Percy's genius was finally recognized.

In 1954, he established his own laboratory, Julian Laboratories, and when he sold it several years later it made him one of the first black millionaires in America. In 1973, holding 130 chemical patents, he was elected to the National Academy of Sciences.

It was because of Percy's dogged perseverance and ingenuity that many of today's commonly used therapeutic drugs, including steroids and birth control pills, are available and affordable. He was inducted into the National Inventors Hall of Fame in 1990.

"I don't think that you can possibly embrace the kind of joy which one who has worked with plants and plant structures such as I have over a period of nearly 40 years, how wonderful the plant laboratory seems."

Percy Julian

Joe Mitty

Born: May 7, 1919, London, U.K.
Died: September 30, 2007, Oxford, U.K.

Joe Mitty was an entrepreneur and salesman who was responsible for turning one Oxfam shop into a national network of charity shops.

After his father's death, when Joe was just ten years old, he was raised in London by his mother. He showcased his entrepreneurial side early when, in his first job, he convinced people to buy old orange cartons for use as firewood.

Joe attended school at Pitman's College, where he studied administration and bookkeeping, before going on to join the Territorial Army. It was in 1942, when he was sent to India on service duty, that he suddenly found himself confronted by the realities of poverty for those living in the slums of Calcutta. He became determined to make as much money as possible for those who needed it the most.

A few years on, after time working for the Ministry of Defense, Joe answered a job ad for what was then called the Oxford Committee for Famine Relief. He became the charity's first paid worker, overseeing their accounts and sending donations of clothes from Britain to those affected by war abroad. But then Joe had an idea. Instead of sending the clothes abroad, he realized there was more potential in selling the donations in a shop and sending the profits overseas. Joe set up Oxfam's first "charity shop" in Oxford in 1949.

His ideas caused a revolution in the retail sector. By the 1960s, he had helped open even more Oxfam shops around the U.K. With his excellent salesmanship, he was able to sell anything from books to a donkey and even a houseboat for the charity. He also used the media to bring the plight of those affected by famine, war, and floods to the attention of the public. Oxfam went on to become the biggest charity retailer on the high street, and many other charities soon followed suit.

Even after retiring from Oxfam in 1982, Joe—nicknamed "salesman of the angels"—helped inspire and mentor the 20,000 volunteers who work in the charity's 700 shops. In 2000, he received an Order of the British Empire (MBE) for his work, and later a lifetime achievement award for ITV's Pride of Britain event. Determined to make the world a better place, Joe's entrepreneurial spirit had made it possible for Oxfam to raise £500 million in under 60 years to help people in need around the world.

"I had two words—rage and passion. Rage because of the inequality and injustice in the world, and a passion to do something about it."

Emily Davison

Born: October 11, 1872, London, U.K.
Died: June 8, 1913, Epsom, U.K.

Emily Davison was a militant suffragette who fought for equal voting rights for women.

Emily studied literature at Royal Holloway College and Oxford University at a time when women were not allowed to graduate with degrees. Later, while working as a private teacher for a family in Berkshire, she became involved with the Woman's Social and Political Union (WSPU). This was a movement set up to fight for the right to vote (suffrage) for women in Britain, whose members were known as "suffragettes."

Because of her commitment to the movement, Emily gave up her teaching career to focus on the WSPU. She became increasingly active with her protests and was arrested on many occasions for protest-related offenses, spending months at a time in prison. While in custody, she and other suffragettes would go on hunger strikes in a bid to make the government acknowledge that the crimes they had committed were political acts. This often led to the women being force-fed. However, on one occasion, Emily prevented this by using furniture to barricade herself into her cell. A guard tried to fill her cell with water, but Emily was freed.

By 1911, Emily's protest attempts were becoming increasingly militant and were no longer favored by the WSPU. But she was convinced that they would never get the vote without a martyr, so on June 4, 1913, she made her way to the Epsom Derby, a horse race attended by society's elite. When the horses charged by where she was standing, she "threw herself" in front of King George V's horse. It collided with her at great speed, causing fatal injuries.

Emily's reasons for the act were unclear, with some claiming she was trying to cross the track, while others believed she was trying to pull down the horse. However, newsreel footage from the day showed that she may have actually been trying to pin a WSPU banner to the horse's bridle.

The WSPU gave Emily a large funeral procession, and 6,000 women marched to show their support. The phrase engraved on her headstone read: "Deeds not words." Emily's legacy is controversial, but many salute her for being a brave martyr for women's rights. However, it took another 15 years before the suffragettes finally achieved their goal of winning British women the right to vote.

"*The true militant suffragette is an epitome of the determination of women to possess their own souls.*"

Emily Davison

Vera Deakin White

Born: December 25, 1891, Melbourne, Australia
Died: August 9, 1978, Melbourne, Australia

Vera Deakin White was the founder of the First World War's Australian Wounded and Missing Enquiry Bureau, which hoped to discover the fate of Australian soldiers in the Gallipoli campaign.

Born to a wealthy family, and with a father who went on to become a prime minister of Australia, Vera could have led a life of security and privilege. She studied music at Melbourne University and had good prospects as a concert artist. However, during a visit to London, the First World War broke out and Vera was determined to do something to benefit the war effort. She gathered a group of women together to undertake war work, and upon her return to Australia she trained as a nurse for the Australian branch of the Red Cross.

In 1915, Vera was encouraged to travel to Egypt to join another arm of the Red Cross. The day after her arrival, she got to work setting up and leading a division called the Australian Red Cross Wounded and Missing Enquiry Bureau. The organization aimed to provide information about soldiers to their relatives. Although the news they communicated was often tragic, Vera led her team to relay thousands of messages back home to the soldiers' families.

In 1917, Vera's bureau sent over 27,000 letters to relatives who could not get answers from the military about the fate of loved ones who were missing, wounded, captured, or killed. As one mother pleaded in a letter: "Did he suffer much, and was he conscious, did he ask for his parents in any way and did he send any message… I am so anxious to know all about my dear boy".

For her services leading the bureau, Vera was awarded an Order of the British Empire (OBE) in 1917. When the Second World War broke out, women again worked on both the home front and front lines to help with the war effort. So Vera resurrected the bureau at a time when the Red Cross was Australia's largest charitable organization.

Although Vera went on to focus on many charitable duties throughout the rest of her life, she remained committed to the Red Cross, later becoming its vice chair and an honorary life member. Eager to serve the less fortunate, she co-founded the Victorian Society for Crippled Children and Adults. With a tireless commitment to the war effort, she also helped numerous charities that benefitted those affected by war until her death at the age of 87.

Vera Deakin White

"What we tried to accomplish ... was to relieve as quickly as possible the anxiety of the relatives in Australia ..."

Emmy Noether

Born: March 23, 1882, Erlangen, Germany
Died: April 14, 1935, Bryn Mawr, Pennsylvania

Emmy Noether, was a mathematician who made important contributions to algebra and theoretical physics in the 1900s.

With a mathematics professor for a father, it was perhaps no surprise that Emmy abandoned her traditional studies in arts and languages in favor of mathematics. At that time, because she was a woman she was unable to study mathematics officially at a university, so she attended classes knowing she would not earn a degree. When this situation changed in 1904, Emmy embarked on her mathematics Ph.D.

Emmy first found work at the Institute of Erlangen in Germany, helping her father with research and lecturing whenever he was ill. She had to work without pay or title, but began publishing her own research papers under a man's name. She would go on to publish more than 40 papers, and unearth relationships between numbers and equations that had eluded other mathematicians.

She became well known for her expertise, and in 1915 at Gottingen's Mathematical Institute she was able to lecture for the first time under her real name.

As well as teaching a dedicated group of students who had traveled from as far as Russia, Emmy worked with many of the leading mathematicians of the day on her own theories. Her unique approach to mathematics allowed her to discover some of the basic rules of the universe and she was even able to work on Albert Einstein's famous Theory of Relativity. Yet it would be three years before she would be allowed a salary for her role.

In 1933, the Nazi government dismissed Jews from teaching posts, leaving Emmy no choice but to flee Germany. With the help of Einstein, she took up a position at Bryn Mawr College in Pennsylvania, where she was accorded long overdue respect for her achievements and taught alongside other women for the first time. However, just 18 months later, she died of complications after surgery.

Although Emmy's name remains relatively unknown today, her work—especially "Noether's theorem," as it is called—is often considered the basis for modern physics. Her legacy is twofold: she made huge contributions to the field of mathematics, especially abstract algebra, and she inspired future generations of mathematicians.

"... Noether was the most significant creative mathematical genius thus far produced since the higher education of women began."

– Albert Einstein, in a letter to the *New York Times*.

Arunachalam Muruganantham

Born: Unknown date 1962, Coimbatore, India

Arunachalam Muruganantham is an entrepreneur who invented a simple low-cost sanitary pad-making machine and, in doing so, created jobs and opportunities for rural Indian women.

Muruga grew up innovating low-cost business opportunities and selling anything from fireworks to sugar cane to help supplement his mother's farm-worker income. But later in life, when he saw his wife hiding rags from him to use instead of sanitary pads for menstruation, he faced a new challenge. Hearing that she would not purchase the pads due to their high cost, he set out to find a way to make sanitary pads that were affordable.

His initial efforts fashioning pads from cotton wool and cotton failed, his wife admitting they were useless. Then he tried testing further handmade pads on family members and a group of medical students, but it was too much of a taboo topic for them to give him the feedback he needed. Without any other options, he resorted to wearing the pads and a pretend uterus—made by filling the bladder from a football with goats' blood—himself. Unable to deal with this and the hostile reactions of their community, his wife moved out.

In rural India, women employ all sorts of methods to cope with menstruation, as millions do not have access to safe or affordable sanitary products. Some use ashes, newspapers, or unhygienic cloths, and coping with these challenges sometimes forces young girls to miss or drop out of school.

Unwilling to give up, Muruga pretended to be a textile mill owner and asked for samples of sanitary pads from big brands. After analyzing the samples for two years, he discovered the correct material to use but this raised another problem—the need to design a machine that would breakdown the raw materials and form them into sanitary pads. Four years later, his mini-machine was perfected.

Muruga achieved many awards, and in 2014 was named one of *TIME* Magazine's "100 Most Influential People." Although large companies have offered to buy his machines, he has so far refused, instead selling them to women's self-help groups and schools. This allows them to make affordable sanitary pads, to earn money, and to go to school or work while menstruating. Muruga's determination, invention, and spirit has benefitted millions of women in India and in many developing countries.

"I have accumulated no money but I accumulate a lot of happiness."

Wangari Maathai

Born: April 1, 1940, Ihithe, Kenya
Died: September 25, 2011, Nairobi, Kenya

Wangari Maathai was a professor and activist who became the first African woman to receive a Nobel Peace Prize.

Wangari was one of 300 Kenyans chosen to study in the U.S. While there, she earned a Master of Science degree in Biological Sciences. Wangari was the first woman in east and central Africa to earn a Ph.D., and become an associate professor and the chair of a university department.

Wangari's work as a veterinarian and in volunteer groups took her to the very poorest areas of Africa. It allowed her to notice the link between damage to the environment—such as forests being cleared for commercial plantations—and the struggles of nearby people who were reliant on those sources for water, crops, animal feed, and firewood. So, in 1977, Wangari introduced the idea of community-based tree planting. Starting with just seven trees on the first day, her campaign developed into the Green Belt Movement—an organization that empowers communities, especially the women, to preserve the environment around them. By planting seedlings, a community is conserving its vital resources and earning money for its work.

Soon the tree became a symbol of the poor political management of Kenya's environment. As people planted trees, they educated themselves and became involved in addressing governmental as well as environmental issues. Wangari confronted politicians about land-grabbing activities and even stood up to President Daniel Arap Moi when he tried to build a 62-story building on green space. During many conflicts with the authorities, she was arrested, received death threats, and beaten.

None of these stopped Wangari. In the early 1990s, she became involved in politics and by 2003 was a government assistant minister for environment and natural resources. She later ran a tree-planting program that resulted in seven billion trees being planted around the world.

In 2004, Wangari received the Nobel Peace Prize for her "contribution to sustainable development, democracy, and peace." She traveled the world to promote her environmental and political ideas until her death from ovarian cancer in 2011. With her Green Belt Movement as an ongoing legacy, she is remembered as a fearless activist determined to challenge leaders to do more for the environment.

Wangari Maathai

"It's the little things citizens do. That's what will make the difference. My little thing is planting trees."

53

Sojourner Truth

Born: around 1797, Rifton, New York
Died: November 26, 1883, Battle Creek, Michigan

Sojourner Truth was an African American activist who fought for women's rights and the abolition of slavery in the U.S.

Born into a family of slaves, Sojourner was one of 12 children. When their owner died, Sojourner was sold with a flock of sheep at an auction. She would be sold twice more over the following years.

While a slave in New York State, Sojourner fell in love with a man from a neighboring farm. She gave birth to a daughter but the man's owner prevented the couple from seeing each other again. She was later made to marry another slave by her owners, with whom she had more children.

In 1826, Sojourner escaped from slavery with one of her daughters, Sophia. Her other daughter and five-year-old son, Peter, had stayed behind and she later heard that he had been illegally sold to a man in another state. Sojourner went to court to gain Peter's freedom, and she became one of the first black women to win a case against a white man in a U.S. court. Peter stayed with his mother until adulthood, when he took a job on a whaling ship. It was the last time Sojourner ever saw her son.

Sojourner worked as a housekeeper for various families, but also used her freedom to fight for worthy causes. In 1844, she moved in with a self-sufficient community that supported women's rights. She began touring to speak against slavery and addressed audiences, including the first National Women's Rights Convention in Massachusetts, about human rights. Sojourner gained prominence as a former slave, and one of her most famous speeches, "Ain't I a Woman?," spoke directly to the issues of racial and sexual inequality.

Other subjects Sojourner championed included improving prison conditions and offering land grants to former slaves so they could become independent. When the Civil War broke out, she called for black troops to be recruited into the Union army and volunteered to take them food and clothing. Her experiences and firmly held views led her to meet with President Abraham Lincoln.

When Sojourner died, her funeral was the biggest the town of Battle Creek had seen. She used her freedom to dedicate her life to many worthwhile causes and has an overlooked place in history as an early leader in the fight for human rights.

"*I will not allow my life's light to be determined by the darkness around me.*"

Beatrice Tinsley

Born: January 27, 1941, Chester, U.K.
Died: March 23, 1981, New Haven, Connecticut

Beatrice Tinsley was an astronomer and cosmologist who contributed to our knowledge of how galaxies change over time.

Although born in England, her family moved to New Zealand when she was young. She was an excellent student and decided at the age of 14 that she wanted to be an astrophysicist. After winning a scholarship to Canterbury University, in New Zealand's south island, she earned a Masters degree and married a fellow student in 1961.

Her husband's career took them to Dallas, in the U.S., but Beatrice was unable to find work in that city, so she had to take a part-time teaching job at the University of Texas in Austin, over 200 miles (320 km) away. In addition to the commute, raising two adopted children, and teaching, she managed to complete her Ph.D. in record time, studying when the children were asleep.

Beatrice's Ph.D. thesis and research became legendary among scientists. At this time, scientists were only just realizing the scale of the universe, and Beatrice's research proposed new ways of working out how far away distant galaxies were.

Her ideas helped scientists learn about how big the universe was and how fast it was growing. She also realized that it was possible to use existing knowledge of stars to work out how galaxies looked.

Beatrice's research led to a prize from the American Astronomical Society in 1974, but she was still unable to get any professional respect in Dallas. Eventually, she decided to forfeit her marriage and moved across the country to Yale University where she could get the recognition she deserved. There, she became a professor of astronomy and a world leader in the field. She published more than 100 papers and became a mentor to other female scientists. However, just six years later, she died of cancer at just 41 years old.

In 1981, her name was preserved forever when an asteroid was named after her, and later a New Zealand mountain. Although she is mostly unknown outside academic circles today, Beatrice was one of science's most original thinkers. Her discoveries have had an enormous impact on our understanding about the origin and size of the universe and laid the foundations for one of the most important theories of our time—the Big Bang theory.

Beatrice Tinsley

"I used to read the encyclopedia as a kid and wish I could understand and contribute to cosmology."

Martti Ahtisaari

Born: June 23, 1937, Viipuri, Finland (now Vyborg, Russia)

Martti Ahtisaari is a politician who has played a vital role in peace deals around the world.

Ahtisaari was born in a Finnish town that sat near the border with Russia at the time. However, when the Soviet Union invaded Finland, in what became the Winter War of 1939–40, the town was taken over and his family driven out. They moved from place to place, before settling in the Finnish city of Oulu, where Ahtisaari completed his education. This experience had a marked impact on him, giving him sympathy for displaced people and motivating him in his pursuit of world peace.

After training in the military and as a teacher, he spent some time working on an educational project in Pakistan, before joining Finland's Foreign Ministry in 1965. As a representative of the United Nations (UN), he worked to bring countries together to resolve conflicts and went on to spend the majority of his career negotiating for peace in various trouble spots around the world. A crucial moment in his career was when he oversaw Namibia's independence from South Africa in 1989–90, restoring peace after 24 years of guerilla war that created over 75,000 refugees.

Between 1994 and 2000, he served as the president of Finland and used his position to lead Finland to join the European Union, potentially saving the country from economic failure. He was instrumental in ending the war in Kosovo in 1999, by negotiating with President Slobodan Miloševic of Yugoslavia to accept a peace plan. Another notable achievement was his setting up of the Crisis Management Initiative (CMI) in 2000, which works to prevent and resolve violent conflicts. This Finnish organization played an important part in ending a 30-year war with a 2005 peace accord between Indonesia and the group known as the Free Aceh Movement.

In 2008, Ahtisaari won the Nobel Peace Prize "for his important efforts, on several continents and over more than three decades, to resolve international conflicts." He later joined The Elders, a group brought together by Nelson Mandela, Graca Machel, and Desmond Tutu, to work with global leaders for peace and human rights.

Ahtisaari is still a peace negotiator, and has received awards and honors from almost every country in the world but he remains confident that all countries could one day achieve peace.

Martti Ahtisaari

"Wars and conflicts are not inevitable. They are caused by human beings."

Abbé Pierre

Born: August 5, 1912, Lyon, France
Died: January 22, 2007, Paris, France

Abbé Pierre was a priest, humanitarian, and the founder of the homeless charity Emmaus.

Pierre, born Henri Grouès, became a Roman Catholic priest in 1938 but when the Second World War broke out in France, he changed his name and joined the French Resistance. He would prepare fake identity papers and helped smuggle Jews from France into Switzerland.

After the war, Pierre was elected to be a member of the National Assembly. But his political duties were overshadowed by a desire to confront the miseries he saw in the lives of the homeless around him. So, in 1949, he founded what would become the Emmaus homeless charity.

However, he saw the idea of charity in a different light to others. Instead of asking the rich to give gifts to the poor, his vision was to develop communities that could be helped to help themselves. The first person to benefit from Pierre's charity was Georges, whom Pierre asked to help him build temporary homes for those in need. As Georges said: "What I was missing, and what he offered, was something to live for."

The charity did not truly take off until 1954, during a particularly cold winter in France. Pierre learned of a homeless woman who had died of hypothermia on the streets, so he wrote angry open letters to the press, as well as speaking on the radio, to shame the government into action. They responded by setting up emergency centers. Support for Pierre's charity grew overnight.

Pierre became an unofficial spokesperson for the homeless. Although admired by Catholics for his positive representation of Catholic faith, he was also loved by anti-Catholics, as he spoke out in favor of things such as homosexuality and contraception. In the final years of his life he was repeatedly voted France's most popular man in public opinion polls. He received the Legion of Honour award and then, in 2004, the Grand Cross, France's highest award. He had refused the Legion of Honour in 1992, as he disapproved of the government's policies for the homeless.

Pierre spoke out for those less fortunate than himself until his death at the age of 94, and the Emmaus charity—his legacy—now has a presence in 36 countries, across four continents.

"People are needed to take up the challenge, strong people, who proclaim the truth, throw it in people's faces, and do what they can with their own two hands."

More Unsung Heroes

The unsung heroes in this book represent a tiny selection of men and women who deserve recognition for their selfless efforts. Throughout history and in every country, there have been individuals who dedicated themselves to causes. Here are some more unsung heroes:

Nicholas Winton

Born: May 19, 1909, London, U.K.
Died: July 1, 2015, Slough, U.K.

Nicholas Winton could not ignore the plight of Jews being persecuted by the Nazis, so in 1938 he headed to Prague, in Czechoslovakia. With the assistance of two colleagues, Nicholas arranged eight trains to carry 669 Jewish children to the U.K., having already arranged foster care for each child and battled with government bureaucracy. Nicholas was knighted in March 2003.

Maria-Feodorovna Romanov

Born: November 26, 1847, Copenhagen, Denmark
Died: October 13, 1928, Klampenborg, Denmark

Born Princess Dagmar of Denmark, she took the name Maria-Feodorovna Romanov when she became the wife of Russia's Alexander III. On the death of Alexander III, the tsarina found warrants, bearing her husband's signature, with the names of criminals and traitors and their fates. On one warrant, Alexander had written: "Pardon impossible, to be sent to Siberia." Alexander, a repressive ruler, had exiled thousands to Siberia's long, harsh winter, where the chances of death were high. But, if this story is proven true, the tsarina showed herself to be a more humane ruler when she changed the punctuation on her husband's note to: "Pardon, impossible to be sent to Siberia" thus saving a life.

Charlotte Sorkine Noshpitz

Born: February 15, 1925, Paris, France

As a member of the French Resistance during the Second World War, Charlotte, aged only 17, accompanied groups of children from Nice, in the south of France, to the Swiss border and safety. She helped make false identity papers and, for the Jewish Fighting Organization, moved weapons to where they were needed. For her bravery and active role in the liberation of Paris, she received many honors and awards.

Bob Bartlett

Born: April 20, 1904, Seattle, Washington
Died: December 11, 1968, Cleveland, Ohio

Bob Bartlett is most remembered for taking on the cause of statehood for Alaska. He entered the political world after completing his schooling and served in a number of positions for the territory of Alaska before committing himself to the struggle of making Alaska—the ignored colony—the 49th state of the Union. The journey to statehood took some 20 years, with admission to the Union declared in 1959. Bob became Alaska's first senator, taking on issues such as the infant mortality rate, tuberculosis, and poverty in the native population. He had a record number of bills passed. Bob was described as a person of "high vision, lofty idealism, prodigious energy, and sacrificial devotion."

Pastor Lee Jong-rak

Born: September 5, 1954, South Korea

At this pastor's church in Seoul, South Korea, is a "baby box" where unwanted babies are left, preventing, says Lee, the infants from being killed, or abandoned, and left to die on the streets. Since the box was installed in 2009, 383 children have been left to be transferred to an orphanage. Though his motives are honorable, there is growing opposition to Lee's work, saying that it not only allows but encourages parents to abandon their infant children. Lee is undeterred and is planning another church with a baby box.

Eugene Lazowski

Born: Unknown date 1913, Czestochowa, Poland
Died: December 16, 2006, Eugene, Oregon

Known as "the Polish Schindler," Eugene was a soldier in the Polish army, a Catholic and a doctor during the Nazis 1939–45 occupation of Poland. His neighbors, many of them Jewish, would hang a rag over his fence and he would make a house call, risking his life. But his and a colleague's greatest act was when they injected Jews and non-Jews in the Rozwadow ghetto with a vaccine containing dead epidemic typhus. The injected suffered no side effects, but when tested by the Nazis, the results read as positive for typhoid. The Nazis quarantined the ghetto and deportations were stopped, meaning that Eugene had saved over 8,000 people from Nazi concentration camps and the gas chambers.

Alice Catherine Evans

Born: January 29, 1881, Neath, Pennsylvania
Died: September 5, 1975, Arlington, Virginia

Alice Evans was an American scientist whose work on disease-causing (pathogenic) bacteria in dairy products was groundbreaking. In 1918, Alice discovered that a bacteria, later to be named brucellosis, found in raw milk could cause spontaneous abortions in animals and fever in humans. Other scientists and veterinarians, doctors and the dairy industry were highly critical of her claim and her recommendation that milk be pasteurized (heat-treated) to kill the bacteria. She contracted chronic brucellosis in 1922, and it recurred throughout her life. Pasteurization was legislated in the 1930s in the U.S., and in 1993, this resolute, pioneering scientist was inducted into the National Women's Hall of Fame.

Eugene Cernan

Born: March 14, 1934, Chicago, Illinois

Eugene Cernan was a captain in the U.S. Navy until selected to be a NASA astronaut in 1963. He flew on three missions—Gemini IX, Apollo 10, and Apollo 17—and logged 566 hours and 15 minutes in space, of which 73 hours were spent on the Moon. It was on the Apollo 17 mission in 1972 that Eugene became the last man to leave his footprints on the Moon's surface. The film, *The Last Man on the Moon*, celebrates his life.